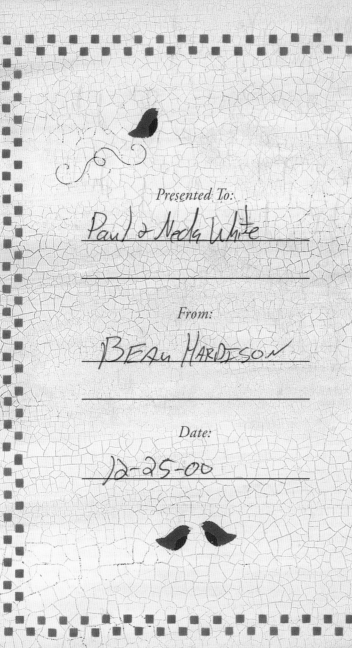

Presented To:

Paul & Neda White

From:

BEAU HARDISON

Date:

12-25-00

Dear
Paul & Neda,
There is nothing like
Country Blessings except
the Blessings of Love and True
Friendship. Thanks for your Blessing
of Love and your true Friendship.
May your Home be Filled with all the
Country Blessing's you desire.
Merry Christmas
Love
BEAU
OO'

Country
Blessings®

Honor Books
Tulsa, Oklahoma

Country Blessings®

ISBN 1-56292-820-1

Illustrations by Heather Solum

Design by Lori Jackson

Copyright 2000 © by Honor Books

P.O. Box 55388

Tulsa, Oklahoma 74155

Country Blessings® is a registered trademark of Sierra Gift Company.

Hearts & Homes
are
warmed by Love.

Let
all you
do
be done
in
Love.

I Corin. 16:14

Lend a Hand

I am only one,

But still I am one.

I cannot do everything,

But still I can do something

And because I cannot do everything

I will not refuse to do something

that I can do.

— EDWARD EVERETT HALE

Praises we give,
for the bounties of
Fall...
but the harvest of
Friendship
is blest above all.

A THANKSGIVING JOURNAL

A single mother worried that Thanksgiving would get lost in the hubbub of Halloween and the glitter of the Christmas season. From the time her daughter was very small, they kept a daily log of "Things We Are Grateful For" throughout the month of November.

At first it was easy to come up with entries, but soon mother and daughter found they had to pause and think up a new entry each day for their list. Over the years, entries included everything from "my school's playground" and "my driver's license" and "my mom's new job" to "my church youth group," "my kitty, Patches," "big piles of autumn leaves," and "warm chocolate chip cookies."

But best of all, the journal holds pages and pages of names. People whose lives touched the mother and daughter. "Grandma and Grandpa," "my new dad," "Aunt Debbie," and the endless string of "my best friends"—Bonnie, Rachel, Lindsay, Abigail, Caleb, Sean, Ashley.

The list goes on and on. Tucked in the pages of the Thanksgiving Journal are precious memories of friendships forever cherished.

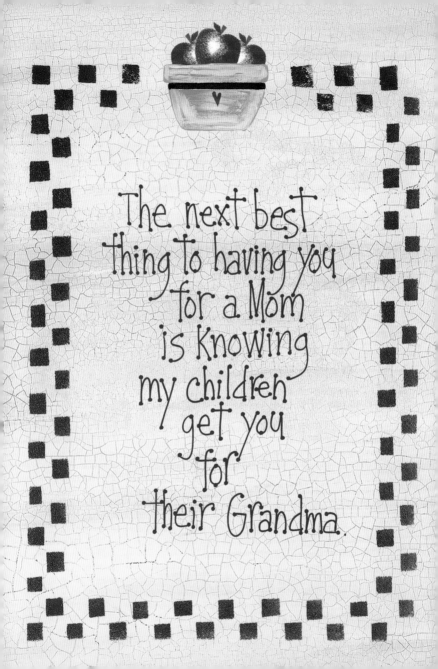

By wisdom

a house is built,

And by understanding

it is established;

And by knowledge the

rooms are filled

With all precious and

pleasant riches.

PROVERBS 24:3-4 NASB

GOD HAS GIVEN
ME ANOTHER DAY

To hear the wonders
He has spoken ...
To see the beauty of
His face ...
To enjoy the pleasure
of His company...
To walk the pathways
of His grace...
To know the delight of
His presence ...
To fulfill the desires
of His Heart...
To discover the treasures
of His Love ...
What a day this will be!

— Roy Lessin

Friends given by God
in mercy and in love;
My counsellors, my comforters,
and guides;
My joy in grief.
My second bliss in joy;
Companions of my young desire;
in doubt
My oracles;
my wings in high pursuit.

O, I remember,
and will never forget
Our meeting spots,
our chosen sacred hours,
Our burning words,
that utter'd all the soul,
Our faces beaming
with unearthly love;
Sorrow with sorrow sighing,
hope with hope
Exulting,
heart embracing heart entire.

— ROBERT POLLOK

Friends
are
the
spice of
Life.

True happiness consists
not in the multitude of friends,
but in their worth and choice.

— Samuel Johnson

We're just a group
of Snowfolk
not made from above.
But you are
God's creation
Handshaped by
His Love.

16

POSITIVE
BOMBARDMENT

The leader gave instructions to the circle of college students: "We'll start with Joyce, and one by one we'll tell her what we like about her, while Joyce quietly listens. Two rules: whatever you say has to be true, and it has to be positive. Then we'll do the same for every girl in the room." Negative comments, kidding, and teasing were not allowed.

"I wish I had hair as pretty as yours."

"You are so smart. I could never keep a 4.0 like you do."

"Everybody wants to be your friend."

"I've never heard you say anything mean about anyone."

"You always make me laugh. When I'm down, I come looking for you."

"Thanks for being there for me when my dad died last year. I don't know how I would have made it without you."

Amid laughter, tears, smiles, and hugs, the girls discovered how special each one is —and how much their lives were touched by one another. Years later they remember that special night when they celebrated their unique gifts.

I Chose my Love.
I Love my Choice.

Someone asked me

To name the time

Our friendship stopped

And love began.

Oh my darling, That's the secret.

Our friendship

Never stopped.

— LOIS WYSE

Good
friends
and
Special
times...

*Grief can take care of itself, but
to get the full value of a joy, you must
have somebody to divide it with.*

— MARK TWAIN

... make
the
best
memories.

Pleasant words are as Honeycomb.

Proverbs 16:24

Kind words can be short and easy to speak, but their echoes are truly endless.

— Mother Teresa

Kindness

is the sunshine

in which

virtue grows.

— R.G. INGERSOLL

23

A Teacher's Love can be felt for a lifetime.

I will instruct you

(says the Lord) and guide you

along the best pathway

for your life; I will advise you

and watch your progress.

PSALMS 32:8 TLB

A teacher affects eternity;
he can never tell where his influence stops.
— Henry Adams

God
cares for
His Creation—
the birds
and lilies, too—

He sees to
every detail
and
He'll provide
for you!

Give thanks to the LORD,
for he is good;
his love endures forever.

PSALM 118:1

A caring nod,

A listening ear,

That's why we hold

Grandmas dear.

A giving heart,

A servant's way,

Joys that last

throughout the day.

Grandmas bring
memories
to our Hearts
and
love to our lives

Faith grows
from
little seeds
of
Hope.

Jesus said:
"Truly I say to you, if you have
faith the size of a mustard seed,
you will say to this mountain,
'Move from here to there,'
and it will move; and nothing will
be impossible to you."

MATTHEW 17:20 NASB

BIG CATCH

"Grandpa is taking me fishing!" five-year-old Lili cried, her excited voice piercing the pre-dawn stillness. Lili's mother groaned as she buried her head under the pillows. This was supposed to be a restful weekend, but apparently Grandpa was too busy making memories to worry about sleep.

Thundering through the house, Lili hurriedly dressed, prayed fervently that she'd get a big catch, slurped down her cereal, and tore out the door for her first fishing expedition. Hours passed, and Lili's mother waited for the pair to return. Beaver Lake in the Arkansas Ozarks was usually a good fishing spot, but it was especially hot and the fish weren't biting. Lili's mother wondered whether her enthusiastic daughter could muster the silence and patience needed for a good catch. What if she didn't catch anything?

But Lili was anything but disappointed. Her eyes beamed with pride as she held up the two small sunfish she had caught. She didn't care that the fish were tiny and boney and hard to eat. To her, they were enormous and delicious, and fishing was a wonderful adventure with her grandpa, her hero. Those two fishes represented a miracle of biblical proportions as her Heavenly Father and earthly grandfather joyfully made a little girl's dreams come true. "Grandpa says I'm the best fisher in the whole wide world!"

The next best thing to having you for a Dad is knowing my children get you for their Grandpa.

Sleep Peacefully,
God is awake..

And be sure of this: I am with you always,

Work Faithfully,
God is your reward.
Live Confidently,
God is in Control.

Roy Lessin

even to the end of the age. Matthew 28:20 NLT

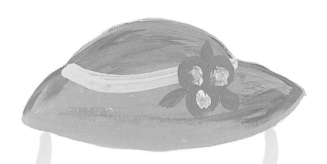

First my Mother
now
my Friend.

Her children arise and call her blessed.

PROVERBS 31:28

All that I am or hope to be,
I owe to my angel mother.
— Abraham Lincoln

A Good neighbor is a Welcome Blessing.

Friendships are

possible only when we

open the window

of our heart and allow

the sunshine of

someone's life in.

— GINNY HOBSON AND
SHERRY MORRIS

My friend you
are in my Heart
whether near
or far apart.

A friend loveth at all times.

Proverbs 17:17 KJV

In every friend we lose a part of ourselves,
and the best part. — *Alexander Pope*

Families
are
like
Quilts~

42

Lives pieced
together
Stitched with
smiles
and tears,
Colored with memories
and
bound by Love.

Show me your ways, O LORD,
teach me your paths; guide me in
your truth and teach me.

PSALM 25:4–5

Education is

not the filling

of a pail,

but the lighting

of a fire.

— William Butler Yeats

A
Teacher
takes a hand
opens a mind,
touches
a Heart.

Trust in the LORD with all your heart and lean not on your own understanding — in all your ways acknowledge him, and he will make your paths straight.

Proverbs 3:5-6

I was young
and now I am old,
yet I have
never seen the
righteous forsaken
or their children
begging bread.

PSALM 37:25

Bless all those who gather here.

The house of the righteous stands firm.

PROVERBS 12:7

May the road rise to meet you,

May the wind be always at your back,

May the sun shine warm upon your face,

The rains fall soft upon your fields and,

Until we meet again,

May God hold you in the palm of His hand.

— Irish blessing

A true friend
warms you
with her
presence,
trusts you with
her
secrets,

and remembers you in her prayers.

Dear friend, I am praying that all is well with you and that your body is as healthy as I know your soul is.

3 JOHN 2 NLT

WRAPPED WITH LOVE

Under the Christmas tree, a man found a huge—but surprisingly light—gift from his three-year-old daughter. He began unwrapping the gift while his little girl watched in wide-eyed wonder. She had wrapped it herself and apparently had used several rolls of Christmas paper to cover the box. He unraveled the first layer of clumsily wrapped paper, then another and another and another.

With each layer, his annoyance grew at this unprecedented waste of perfectly good wrapping paper. He sighed as he finally uncovered a plain brown box. There in long ribbons, were layers of tape strapped across the box openings. He cut through the tape, opened the box, and looked inside. It was empty.

In exasperation, he said, "That is a waste of paper to do this. You don't wrap empty boxes and put them under a Christmas tree. It's not a gift unless there is something actually inside the box."

Undaunted by the rebuke, the little girl replied, "Oh Daddy, the box *isn't* empty! Just before I closed the box, I blew in lots and lots of kisses for you."

Out of
difficulties
grow
miracles.

The problem of crossing the sea

Troubled Moses less

than it would me;

Neither aircraft nor ship

Was required for the trip,

Which he'd booked through

the best Agency.

— D.R. BENSEN

If you don't expect the unexpected,
you will not find it. — Heraclitus

~ Marriage ~

Beloved, let us love one another:
for love is of God;
and every one that loveth is born of God,
and knoweth God.

1 JOHN 4:7 KJV

Joy is the start
of it~
Sharing is part
of it~
Love is the Heart
of it.

A Friend is God's way of walking alongside.

The LORD has sent me

to comfort those who mourn....

He sent me to give them

flowers in place of their sorrow,

olive oil in place of tears,

and joyous praise in place of

broken hearts.

ISAIAH 61:2-3 CEV

In my Father's House
are many mansions~
I hope yours is next
to mine.

"For I know the plans

I have for you,"

declares the LORD,

"plans to prosper you and

not to harm you,

plans to give you hope

and a future."

JEREMIAH 29:11

Whoever sows
generously will also
reap generously.

2 CORINTHIANS 9:6

Cultivate those who can
teach you. — *Baltasar Gracián*

To Teach is
to Touch
a
Life
Forever

A Mother
is
Someone

Who can take
the place
of all others
but whose
place no one
else can
take.

♥ ♥ ♥

Who can find a virtuous woman? for her price *is* far above rubies.

PROVERBS 31:10 KJV

From one small
seed of
kindness....
friendship grows.

SURPRISE FRIENDS

Rose never dreamed that a "chance" business meeting would evolve into a close friendship. She and Ann met in the midst of negotiating a business deal. They assumed this was just a professional relationship, but God had a different plan.

Over the next few years, Rose often thought of Ann, who lived across the country. She frequently prayed for Ann and sent personal notes of encouragement and comfort to Ann, wondering why she was sending scriptures to a woman she barely knew. When their business paths crossed in another country, Ann took the plunge and changed the conversation from business to personal matters. She confided, "Rose, you couldn't know this, but all this time that you've been praying for me, my life was literally in danger." Wide-eyed, Rose listened as Ann shared her deeply personal, tragic story about a violent boyfriend—and thankfully, the happy ending of a new man in her life. Amid laughter and tears, the women struck a bond of shared past hurts and bright hopes for the future.

Over the next few years, the tables were turned as Ann translated her thankfulness into fervent prayers for Rose to find her own Mr. Right. God answered. Ann and her new husband were honored guests at Rose's wedding.

"Ann lives a thousand miles away," Rose said, "and we seldom get to see one another. But Ann always feels close, here in my heart."

This is the day which the Lord hath made; We will rejoice and be glad in it.

Ps. 118:24 KJV

How can I say thanks

for the things You have done for me?

Things so undeserved,

yet You gave to prove Your love for me.

The voices of a million angels

could not express my gratitude.

All that I am

and ever hope to be,

I owe it all to Thee.

— ANDRAÉ CROUCH

69

Grandmas
are just antique
little girls.

If I could search

for one true friend

and seek until the very end,

I'd find out what

I always knew,

there is no better friend than you!

— Roy Lessin

Teach the older women to live
in a way that is appropriate for someone
serving the LORD. . . . These older women
must train the younger women.

TITUS 2:3-4 NLT

In the desert a fountain

is springing,

In the wide waste there

still is a tree,

And a bird in the

solitude singing,

Which speaks to my

spirit of thee.

— LORD BYRON

Live Well
Laugh Often
Love Much !

STARTING OVER

Edward never dreamed that in midlife he would face divorce, a corporate downsize, serious family illness, bankruptcy, and major medical problems of his own—all within the same year. Since his youth, he had believed that if he worked hard, trusted God, and did his best, all things would work out fine. But life had not turned out quite like he had expected.

"Lord, I know You have a plan in all of this," he murmured in prayer. "Show me how to be grateful for what I do have." God heard. The next morning when Edward awoke, his first thought was, *Thank You, Lord, that I am alive, and today is Yours. Do Your will with me.* Day after day, month after month, Edward found many things to be grateful for. His elderly mother's health improved. He made a major career change to work that was infinitely more satisfying—and fun—than anything he had done before. Within a year, he met a woman who made him laugh again. He soon married her, joined a new family, launched a new career, and experienced renewed health.

Life had dealt him a tough hand, but with the tender healing of God's love, Edward found new joy. To this day, his morning prayer remains the same, but he adds a heartfelt postscript as he smiles at his sleeping wife: *And thank You for giving me a whole new life. I never dreamed it could be this good.*

A Mother's
Heart
is a Special
place where
children
always have
a
Home.

As long as I can remember,

As far back as I can see,

My mom has always been there

whenever I'm in need

To hold me tight

when things aren't right,

To calm my fright when things

bump in the night.

She did so much for so little;

She did it all with no complaint

Without my mom to guide me,

Lord knows where I'd be.

That is why my mom is so

beautiful to me.

Faith makes
things possible
not easy!

Every child of God
can defeat the world,
and our faith is what gives
us this victory.

1 JOHN 5:4 CEV

*I never did anything
worth doing by accident,
nor did any of my inventions
come by accident;
they came by work.*
— Thomas Edison

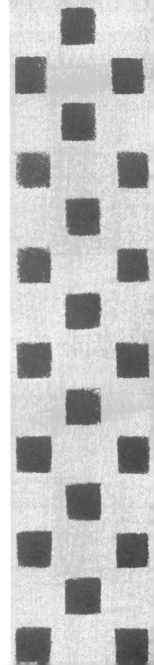

To create a woman

I praise you because I am
fearfully and
wonderfully made.

PSALMS 139:14

God used His
hands
to make a
Mother
God used His
Heart.

A Heart filled
with Love
always has something
to give.

*Those who bring
sunshine to the lives
of others cannot
keep it from themselves.*

— Sir James Barrie

A merry heart doeth good
like a medicine.

Proverbs 17:22 KJV

The
Best
Antiques
are
old
Friends.

God sends each person into this world

with a special message to deliver,

with a special song to sing,

with a special act of love to bestow.

— JOHN POWELL

Sisters
share the
little
things

the joy that Love & Faith can bring.

In the Cookie
of Life ~
Friends are
the
Chocolate Chips.

LOVE BELIEVES THE BEST

One of the noblest friendships in literature is that of Melanie and Scarlett in Margaret Mitchell's classic, **Gone with the Wind.** Melanie is characterized as a woman who "always saw the best in everyone and remarked kindly upon it." Even when Scarlett tries to confess her shameful behavior toward Melanie's husband, Melanie says, "Darling, I don't want any explanation. . . . Do you think I could remember you walking in a furrow behind that Yankee's horse almost barefooted and with your hands blistered— just so the baby and I could have something to eat—and then believe such dreadful things about you? I don't want to hear a word."

Melanie's refusal to believe, or even hear, ill of Scarlett leads Scarlett to passionately desire to keep Melanie's high opinion. It is as Melanie lies dying that Scarlett faces her deep need for Melanie's pure and generous friendship: "Panic clutching at her heart, she knew that Melanie had been her sword and her shield, her comfort and her strength." Melanie had been her only true friend.

There is no
greater
joy than to
know
that my
children
walk with
the
Lord.

You may have tangible wealth untold
Caskets of jewels and coffers of gold;
Richer than I you can never be—
I had a mother who read to me.

— STRICKLAND GILLIAN

Fix these words of mine in your hearts
and minds. . . . Teach them to your children,
talking about them when you sit at home
and when you walk along the road,
when you lie down and when you get up.
Write them on the doorframes of your houses
and on your gates, so that your days
and the days of your children may be many.
Deuteronomy 11:18-21

If friends
were flowers -
I'd pick you!

A friend is a push

when you've stopped…

A word when you're lonely…

A guide when you're searching…

A smile when you're sad…

A song when you're glad.

— GINNY HOBSON AND SHERRY MORRIS

God in His
Goodness,
kindness &
Care....

Gave us a Special friendship to share..

Additional copies of this book
are available from your local bookstore.

If you have enjoyed this book, or if it has
impacted your life, we would like to hear from you.
Please contact us at:

Honor Books
Department E
P.O. Box 55388
Tulsa, Oklahoma 74155

Or by e-mail at info@honorbooks.com